SIMPLE SOLUTIONS

for
Dealing with
Difficult People

5 Simple Habits for Dealing with
Difficult People

Bart Christian

Printed in the United States of America

Christian, Bart
    SIMPLE Solutions for Dealing with Difficult People, 5 Simple Habits for Dealing with Difficult People / by Bart Christian

    ISBN: 978-0-9843263-2-7

Warning – Disclaimer

The purpose of the book is to educate and entertain. The author or publisher does not guarantee that anyone following the techniques, suggestions, tips, ideas, or strategies will become successful. The author and publisher shall have neither liability or responsibility to anyone with respect to any loss or damage caused, or alleged to be caused, directly or indirectly by the information contained in this book.

WHAT OTHERS ARE SAYING

"Great read – quick, concise, to the point and funny. A very simple road map to improving nearly every aspect of your life immediately. Perfect for everyone from the chairman of the board to the worker in the field. Bart has simplified what so many struggle with everyday – How to positively and effectively deal with difficult people and situations.

This book breaks down the 5 habits that once mastered are the gateway to better relationships and improved overall happiness. Thank you Bart, we can all use this book. These are habits we all need to take action on – Today!"

— **"Famous Dave" Anderson, Founder and Owner of "Famous Dave's BBQ" Featured on The Food Network's Hit TV Show, "Best In Smoke"**

"This is a must-read book for anyone wanting the "Simple Solution" to handling difficult people and situations. Bart has effectively put this in terms anyone can grasp and put in to action right now. This will resonate from the boardroom to the break room. Everyone needs this book.

In this book Bart has put together a formula that gives you the opportunity to make the leap to the next level of communication for dealing with difficulty. He boils things down and makes it simple for anyone to get and implement immediately in their life. By following these simple steps you can begin to have the relationships you were always meant to have.

Life is always throwing us curveballs and distractions. If you want to get ahead quickly and effectively this is a must read. Don't just read it – study it and master these 5 simple habits. A brilliantly simple formula for living an extraordinary life! Read it and most importantly TAKE ACTION on it.

You can spend the rest of your life trying to figure out how to better the relationships in your life, or you can follow the proven habits and principals found in this book. It is your choice, do it the hard way . . . or do it the smart way, which is learning from Bart."

— **James Malinchak, Featured on ABC's Hit TV Show, "Secret Millionaire" Co-Author, Chicken Soup for the College Soul Founder, www.BigMoneySpeaker.com**

"Finally! Something simple and not over complicated. Simple habits that we can all identify and make part of our daily routine. Just follow Bart's instructions and you will grow your connection in relationships at home, work and in life."

— **Jonathan Sprinkles, "Your Connection Coach"**
TV Personality, Author, National Speaker of the Year

"What do profound, interesting, funny and imaginative all have in common? The answer is the author of this book, my friend, Bart Christian. I have spent my career showing people and organizations how to do better and be better. That's why I like this book … Bart shows without a doubt that most of us take the wrong approach to dealing with difficult people in work and in life. The best thing about this book is that Bart will give you simple solutions to unravel what can be a complex subject and instead make it exceptionally easy for all to understand. This book will help you turn the most difficult, impossible and unreachable people in your life into the most devoted and loyal colleagues and lifetime friends. No matter what your profession or job title you will benefit from the content in this book. If you want to make a difference in your life then Bart's new book is one that you want on your book shelf."

— **Craig Weidel, SNS, CHt., NLP – 'The Child Nutrition Guy'**
Speaker, Author, Coach, CEO – Speaking Dynamic Concepts, LLC

"I can't tell you what a lifesaver Bart is - he knows what he is talking about and he knows how to keep your interest! When someone knows what they are talking about, believes in the message, people will be sold on the message – thanks Bart!"

— **Karen Johnson Past President, School Nutrition Association School Nutrition Director - Yuma Elementary School District – Yuma, AZ**

"This wonderful and insightful book shows you how to be more persuasive and influential, and get your ideas across faster than ever."

— **Brian Tracy Top selling author of over 45 books, Has Addressed more than 4,000,000 people in 4,000 talks and seminars**

DEDICATION

This is dedicated to my wife Melisa and my children Westley and Olivia Grace. These people, who I love more than anything else in this world, have taught me a great deal about the topic. Not so much in that they were difficult but rather in helping me to see that often times (very often) it was me who was the most challenging to deal with. Their love and faith in me I have never doubted and it has been a rich blessing in my life.

To my good friend Karen Johnson who over the last decade has always encouraged me with the right word at exactly the time I needed it most. She has been an angel in my life. Thank you Karen I am blessed to be considered your friend.

Of course I cannot forget our parents. To my great Mom & Dad who always believed in me even when I did not and to Melisa's parents, "Can you believe it? We made it for over a quarter century."

To my mentor for the last 25 years, Zig Ziglar. His books See You at the Top and Over the Top have been indispensable tools in my positive attitude arsenal. You will see Zig's influence in everything I have written and said over the last 10 years.

Most importantly to God who has blessed my life in every good way with good friends, health and a loving family. I am thankful for the trials, heartaches, laughter, love and joy that have brought me to where I am and continue to mold me daily. All the honor and glory are due Him.

Philippians 4:13

Bart Christian

The Ideal Choice For A Speaker At Your Next Event!

Programs can be tailored to fit your theme of:

Professional Growth,

Personal Development,

Team Building, Coaching

Staff, Leadership, Change,

Motivating Staff, etc.

To Check Availability or for More Information:

Call: 1(888) 838.1550 or
(520) 744.1092

Email: bart@bartchristian.com

www.BartChristian.com

TABLE OF CONTENTS

THANK YOU

In this day we live in it seems that the art of saying "Thank you" has been all but lost and these two words along with "I am sorry" can be game changers in relationships and business. So without wasting another word I want to say thank you to two men who have meant so much to me and my business.

First off to my coach, James Malinchak, "Thank you" for giving me the opportunity to grow on stage and showing me the way through the forest when all I could see were the blades of grass. I am blessed and very proud to call you my friend.

To my long time friend, Lou Volpe, you inspired me in so many ways over the last 20 years. At first from afar and now as my most trusted advisor and one of my closest and dearest friends. I appreciate you and your lovely wife Judy more than words can express.

To Mary Swift, Child Nutrition and Food Services Director with Albuquerque Public Schools, I owe a great deal of thanks to you for allowing me to craft this message as well as the rest of the Simple Solutions series in front of your staff over the last few years. You allowed me to make mistakes, to make course corrections and to come back stronger every time. The feedback you and your staff have given has been invaluable to making this a tool that is useful to anyone who has to deal with others as a part of their vocation or just in the day to day relationships we all enjoy.

I wish there was enough space to list every name of every person in the various School Nutrition Associations nationwide, and especially in Arizona and New Mexico, who had a positive impact on my life and the lives of my family and our entire team. So to all those who may read this who have been good finders and cheerleaders to us over the last decade I would like to offer a sincere thank you for your impact and also say, "I am sorry" there is not more space to list each of you. We thank God for bringing you into our lives and building us up when we needed it most.

FORWARD BY NANCY RICE

As a past president of the national School Nutrition Association I know firsthand the importance of making the right choices when dealing with difficult situations. In this book Bart Christian has given his readers a road map that will equip anyone to be their best. Bart has identified simple habits that everyone can use in their professional and personal relationships that, if applied, will make you happier and more productive no matter the situation.

More than ever these simple habits are needed today as many of our customers and staff are facing unprecedented challenges on the job as well as at home. I am sure that if the habits outlined in this book are put into practice you will see an immediate impact in the form of better relationships and a happier life. These habits will guide you to make the choice today to "Be Your Best" for your customers, your co-workers and most especially for you.

When I first met Bart over 15 years ago who could have guessed the divergent paths our lives were to take. We have both seen great change and blessing in our professional lives as well as personally. Through it all I know that we have shared a common love for and a genuine commitment to the school nutrition industry.

We all understand that healthy attitudes feed our minds and prepare us to serve and our service is essential to the educational experience of the nation's children. We are literally changing the health of our nation, one child at a time. Thank you Bart for giving us a simple plan to be the very best we can be every day.

Sincerely
Nancy D. Rice, Past President, School Nutrition Association, State Director, School Nutrition Division, Georgia Department of Education

PREFACE
WHO IS THE "MOST" DIFFICULT PERSON IN YOUR LIFE?

When I was first asked to present a program on dealing with difficult situations and conflict resolution in the workplace my first thought was, "What was the most difficult situation I have ever faced in any job?" Like you I immediately thought about a co-worker or supervisor that I just "could not" get along with or a customer who was just a "pain in the …well, you know." Seemed to me that my life had been full of "difficult people" and I would have a wealth of experiences from which to pull.

I did what I normally do when assembling information for a talk or presentation, I made a list of personal stories and material that pertained to the topic. As I looked at that list a funny thing started to happen and I credit time as well as advancing years to the revelation. I realized that in a lot of the instances with those "difficult people" I had encountered it was, in many cases, my lack of patience, misunderstanding and/or my unwillingness to listen that caused the difficulty. In fact, in hindsight (which is far better than 20/20) I clearly saw that my stubbornness and over-reaction was the reason for several of the conflicts. Talk about a "slap in the face."

In the last 10 years, I have really been making a study of people and I realized these five things that I am going to share with you. These five things were always right there in front of me and the really crazy thing is they were so obvious and simple. Interestingly I found out that the simple things are not always easy. Also, the simpler something is to do it is equally as simple not to do.

As I was thinking about them, I said, "Okay, what am I going to call them? Am I going to call them tips or ideas? Am I going to call them shortcuts or techniques?" And then I figured this, they are steps. Because a step takes you forward, lifts you to a higher place and often leads to a door. That is exactly what this information is, steps to a door that if you will just open will change the way you look at difficulty and challenge.

So as you read this little volume you will be given some practical and very doable simple steps for dealing with difficulty as it crosses your path every day. You will also be faced with the fact that sometimes the most difficult person you will have to cope with some days is the person you see in the mirror. I make you this promise – If you will make the choice to take these "5 Habits" and implement them into your day and your life you will be a better co-worker, supervisor, mate and friend. No, I take that back it's not a promise…it's a guarantee!! Let's get started.

INTRODUCTION

WE ARE THE CHOICES WE MAKE

I have learned this life is really about making good choices every day and that is where we have to start when talking about dealing with difficult people. You see the bottom line is this, we can all think of something we can do that will negatively affect our life – either in our business or personal relationships. There's always something that you can do that can cause a problem. I mean, I know just the right buttons to push with my wife and my co-workers to push them over the edge.

Okay. Now, let me ask you, "Is there something you can think of that you can do that will have a positive effect on your family, your business or your personal life?" If you are honest with yourself the list can be long and pretty simple. Yet so many times we choose to ignore it. Things like asking your mate out on a date or for a walk, getting to work 15 minutes earlier (or maybe just on time) and waking up 20 minutes earlier every day so you can read something uplifting or have a little quiet time. These are examples of little things that can make a huge difference if we just do them.

Now, we have to agree on a few things here; #1 You are responsible for the above choices, the choice is yours alone. #2 Any choice you make is going to have a consequence. Good or bad, there will be consequences. #3 No one can make these choices for you, they are your responsibility.

So, let's put it all together. We agree that regardless of what your past experiences have been and regardless of what your present circumstances are, there are choices that you can make right now that will positively or negatively affect your family, business or personal life and that choice is yours. When you realize the power that you really have over the choices you make every day and accept responsibility, that's when the real magic starts to happen.

What happens in so many of our lives is that we give away our right to choose for ourselves. We let others make the choices for us – either it's what we listen to on the radio, watch on television, or we allow the crabby attitude or foul situation of someone else take control of our attitude and mood. We let other people make that choice for us rather than making it for ourselves.

We are going to spend the rest of this book talking about just how you can set yourself up to make the best choices possible. Because we both know that dealing with difficult people many times comes down to our making the right choices. The way we choose to deal with a situation or an individual has a great influence on the outcome we enjoy or regret.

TAKE ACTION

Think about a recent difficult situation you were involved in or maybe even witnessed. What were some bad choices that were made by those involved? Write them below

_____

_____

_____

Did the reactions that you witnessed or participated in calm or inflame the situation? Write below how the reactions helped or hurt the situation. Try to be as specific as you can.

_____

_____

_____

_____

In hindsight, what could have been done differently to calm the situation and possibly avoid the conflict altogether?

_____

_____

_____

_____

_____

_____

"You are your Choices."
— Seneca

NOTES

_____

_____

_____

_____

_____

_____

_____

_____

_____

_____

_____

_____

_____

NOTES

_____

_____

_____

_____

_____

_____

_____

_____

_____

_____

_____

_____

_____

_____

CHAPTER 1

HABIT 1
Choose to Be Your Best

Choose to be your best. Sounds simple and easy, right? Well, it's not quite so easy, but it is simple. Let's talk about how simple it is.

I know what you are thinking, at least this was what I thought when I discovered this, "I do choose to be my best, I mean I do not consciously make the decision to be my worst." Really? While I did not "choose" to be my worst, there were many times when I did not choose to be my best.

There are three components to this choice and the first part is choosing to be nice. Now, things are going to happen to us every day, negative and positive. You may be thinking, "But, you don't understand. You don't understand my life and I'm just the kind of person – I'm emotional, my feelings are just out there and I can't control it." Yes, you can. I know you can. You may not believe it but you can, and you know you can. Here's the proof.

Have you ever been in an argument with somebody at home? Be honest. The phone rings and you argue all the way until you pick up the receiver and in your most pleasant voice say,

"Hello." It's a choice. You chose to be nicer to the person on the phone than you were with the person you're talking to – it's a choice. Okay, have you ever been in an argument with a co-worker? The boss walks in and in your most pleasant, professional voice say, "Oh, hello Mr. Smith how are you today." You know, it's a choice. You can be nice. So make the choice, make the choice to be nice. It's just that simple.

The second part is choosing to stay calm. When people say things to you that are inflammatory, insensitive or well just plain stupid take a deep breath (two or three if needed) and make the decision to stay calm. Don't let what's going on in somebody else's head control what's going on in yours. If I come to you and I'm in a bad mood and you're in a great mood, why would you let me infect your great mood? Why not try to infect me with your good mood? Flip it.

It's like when someone cuts you off in traffic. They drive off on their merry way and you're screaming and yelling at them and making gestures, or whatever you do. You allow them to affect your attitude and your day while they do not even know you exist. To say the least it is not productive. Bottom line here is to make a decision right now to only fret over what you can control and don't fret over what you can't control. Accept it and move on. That's the big secret to staying calm.

I was in a grocery store not too long ago and this little old man pushes a grocery cart up and he's got probably a 100 items in his cart. The catch is that he is in the express lane designated for 15 items or less. Well, I happened to walk by and as my daughter and I are standing in the lane next to him a very attractive young lady with a gallon of milk and loaf of bread gets in the express lane behind the old gentleman.

Well you can probably guess what happened next. The young lady proceeds to absolutely lose her mind. Well, she started making snide remarks and then, when the older man leaves, she really lets the store staff have it. She yells at the clerk, asks for the manager and loses twenty minutes of her life making a scene. Now, I hung around just to watch because I thought it was interesting that she had let something that she had literally no control over, control her.

Now, the old gentleman is long gone, he's put his groceries in his car and driving home. Do you think he thought another thought about that woman? The simple answer is, "No." What do you think that young lady thought about for the rest of the day? I'll tell you, that little old man, he owned her mind. She willingly allowed him to take over her mind. To be sure she carried her anger home with her that evening.

Honestly I felt bad for everyone there and especially for anyone who was waiting at home for her. She was gone and I went to the manager afterwards and told him what a wonderful staff he had as well as how clean and well stocked the store always seemed to be. I went over to the clerk who had been berated and complimented him on his patience with that little old man. Took me all of two or three minutes but when I left that store the energy was changed and I am certain those involved felt a little better.

Lastly, choose to be happy. Work to not let the events of the day and they are just that – singular, brief events most of the time. Remember, things are going to happen to you every single day. Some good and some not so good understand this and don't be surprised by it. That fact is that everybody you know is either in a crisis, coming out of a crisis or going into a crisis – everybody. It's just life. So, understand that about yourself. Understand that is just the way it is and it's a lot easier to be happy. Also, if you practice staying calm and being nice being happy is a lot easier.

You see quite often there are things going on in people's lives that we know nothing about and these things bubble up in places like the grocery store or in traffic or on the job. They give themselves over to emotion and you just catch the flak from it. But just because they have decided to have a miserable day does not give them the right or power to do that to you UNLESS you give it to them.

TAKE ACTION

Think back to a time when you really did not "choose to be your best." What could you have done differently? Write down just one thing you could have done to influence the situation positively (if you can think of more go for it).

_____

_____

_____

_____

Can you remember an instance where you allowed the "stinking thinking" of someone else affect your attitude? What happened? How would you handle the situation now?

_____

_____

_____

_____

"Don't let the mess in someone else's head control what goes on in yours."
– Sara Christian
(My Grandmother)

NOTES

_____

_____

_____

_____

_____

_____

_____

_____

_____

_____

_____

_____

_____

NOTES

_____

_____

_____

_____

_____

_____

_____

_____

_____

_____

_____

_____

_____

_____

CHAPTER 2

HABIT 2
Protect Your Attitude

Protecting your attitude should be the most important thing that you do every day. As a matter of fact it should be the very first thing you think about when you rise in the morning and the last thing you think about before you drift off to sleep. Now I know exactly what some of you are thinking, "There are far more important things that should fill this time – things like my family, my faith and my spouse for example. These are much more important." Don't get me wrong these are all important, very important to me and should be to everyone however, consider this, "How much good can you do with any of these if you have a 'crappy' attitude." Think about it, every good or bad thing that happens in your relationship with anyone is determined in large part by YOUR attitude.

So how do you protect your attitude? Let me share something with you that is simple and has been true for thousands of years. The first few minutes of every single day are the most important of your day. You know what the second most important part of everyday is? The last few minutes before you go to sleep, let me explain.

The first 15 minutes of everyday is the most important part and the last 15 minutes is the next most important part. Now, why is that? Because your mind is the most susceptible to suggestion and influence when you first wake up in the morning and then again just before you go to sleep. That's just a scientific and psychological fact.

Now, how many of you watch the news before you go to bed? STOP! You go to bed and the last thing you saw was the worst thing happening in the world. So, when you wake up in the morning, all night long your mind is churning on the worst things in the world. Have you ever just sat up in bed in the middle of the night and for some strange reason just not been able to go back to sleep. In many cases this negative input just before bed is the reason.

Next, you wake up in the morning and you turn on the radio. How many of you flip on the radio or turn the TV back on the news when you wake up in the morning? Just to prove this point I have a question – "Have you ever heard a song on the radio or on TV early in the morning and then ALL DAY that song plays over and over in your mind? You just can't get it to go away. The reason is simple, your mind is very open to suggestion in the morning.

And so, without realizing it you are programming your mind. So you need to be sure that you're putting good things into your mind during this time. Why allow some strangers to choose what will go into your mind before you go to bed? When you first wake up in the morning? Would you allow a stranger to dump garbage in the middle of your living room? Of course not, do not allow it in your mind either.

I started a long time ago, listening to inspirational things – motivational talks, positive audio books or preaching or music. It made a huge difference in the way I looked at life and everyone in it. Not immediately but soon and very suddenly the things that used to routinely cause anxiety and stress no longer did.

I know what you're going to say, you're going to say, "Bart, you don't understand, I'm busy. I've got a job. I've got kids. When I get home at night I don't have time to listen to a motivational speaker or study a motivational program." Join the club, we are all busy and yet we seem to find time for things we value. The trick is not to look at this the way most people do and therefore they do not do it.

Most people think like this – I have got to sit down at the table, open up the book, turn the CD on, put the headphones on and study. This is very important to understand …you don't have to do that, okay? Top achievers in relationships, business and nearly anything you can think of will tell you this little secret. "JUST PLAY IT!" Play it in the background while you work. Play it in the CD player of your car. Play it on your MP3 player while you exercise or walk the dog. Put it in your car radio. You'll get it if you just listen. Decide today to take control of what is being fed into your mind.

Remember this, odds are that there is no way that you can have any effect on what is going on in Iraq, Bosnia, South America or China at the present moment. So why fill your mind with the details of war or salacious antics of celebrities? Aren't the details of your life more important to you?

I read in a recent issue of Success magazine that it is estimated that Americans 12 and older spend over 1500 hours watching TV per year. That averages out to over 4 hours per day. Many are spending almost 25% of their waking hours watching TV. Over 25 hours a week, more than one whole day each week. It equals watching TV for almost two solid months out of every 12. Think about that and it becomes pretty clear why so many find it hard to get ahead in life. Imagine if just half that time were spent on self improvement and education.

Let's not leave out reading and the impact it has on you. A recent Gallup study states that about half the people you know do not read anything other than the newspaper or tabloid magazines. It also pointed out that about a third of adults will never read a book cover to cover after leaving high school. This makes it easy to understand the truth in the old saying that "Readers are Leaders.

Here's another interesting fact, if you read just 15 minutes a day that equals one to two books per month and 12 to 20 books per year. That is just 15 minutes …imagine if you did that in the morning AND in the evening. Everything just doubled to 20 + books every year. You could be wiser, smarter and incredibly impactful in your family, community and workplace as long as you were reading the right stuff.

Now don't get me wrong I love a good novel as much as anyone you just do not want your reading diet to focus on anything other than what you want to be or do in your life. An occasional date with a romance, mystery or sci-fi book is great as long as it is just that "occasional." Remember the goal is to protect your attitude and self motivation.

In this technological age getting the information contained in books has never been easier. Your local library has resources that can meet every need for improving. There are obviously books and there are also audio books on CD that you can listen to as you go back and forth to work or driving to the grocery store, etc.

The U.S. Census Bureau says the average drive time for American's to the workplace is a little over 24 minutes. That is 100 hours spent each year commuting to work. The average audio book is around six to eight hours, that means that if you use your car, in the words of Zig Ziglar, as a "classroom on wheels" you can listen to another 10 to 12 books a year just while you drive. Combine this with what you read and you will have absorbed more information and read more than most college graduates.

TAKE ACTION

What is your plan to protect the first 15 minutes of each day? Be specific.

_____

_____

_____

What is your plan to protect the last 15 minutes of each day? Be specific.

_____

_____

_____

What will be the next book you will read? The next audio program you listen to? (For suggestions see the "Reading List" in the Appendix section of this book.)

_____

_____

_____

"Twenty years from now you will be more disappointed by the things you didn't do than by the ones you did do. So throw off the bowlines. Sail away from safe harbor. Catch the trade winds in your sails. Explore … Dream … Discover.
– Mark Twain

BONUS SECTION

I am a firm believer that everybody deserves a little something extra, so is it okay if I give you a little bonus? I thought so. Just to give an illustration on how powerful a good book or in my case a timely audio program can be and just how impactful it can be on you and everyone around you.

Recently I was in Las Vegas participating as a vendor in a trade show exhibition. On the flight to get there I listened to an audio program by one of my mentors and motivation legend Zig Ziglar (*Side note here – Zig is AWESOME I recommend anything he has ever done).* In the program a story about something that happened to him once when his flight was cancelled and how he handled it. As I listen I'm laughing because its a good story and I wondered what I would have done in the same situation. Little did I know that I was going to get the answer to that question very soon.

So, I go to the trade show and do my thing. If you have never been to any type of trade show here is how it goes. The vendors are kind of trapped in this 10 X 10 cubicle and they're sort of walking around like caged animals for up to three days. Everyone is trying to get the attention of those passing by so that they will come take at look at their wares. Well, it is very exhausting and when it is over everyone is ready to go home.

By the end of the show I was no different. My feet were hurting and I was ready to go home. When the show concluded I had my bags together and I sped out to the airport. When I get there (a full hour and half early) I grab a seat beside the gate check-in counter. Just as I get relaxed there is an announcement, "Would everybody on flight # 408 from Las Vegas to Tucson, please report to the check-in counter." Well, since I am sitting right beside it I'm first in line.

Well, that little lady looks at me. She's a cute little girl about 20 to 23 years old and she has got a real deer in the headlights look on her face. I mean she is looking really scared. She looks at me, takes a big gulp and says, "Sir, I'm sorry to tell you but your flight has been cancelled."

I looked at her, sighed a little and said, "Great!" She looked puzzled and replied, "Great?" To which I replied, "Yeah, great!"

She looked at me, still with that deer in the headlights look and asked, "How do you figure it's great?" I proceeded to explain just as I had heard Zig just 3 days before, "Well, I figure it like this. There are only three reasons why they don't fly a plane. Because there's problem with the plane, there's problem with the pilot or there's problem in the air. Either way, I'm doing just fine right here."

That cute little girl then smiled and said, "Well sir, it truly is not that great."

"What do you mean?", I asked and she said, "Well, the next flight is not for over three hours." So there I was in the airport looking at an over four and half hour delay to my flight.

So, I leaned back and asked myself what would Zig do and I replied to her with enthusiasm, "FANTASTIC!"

That little lady went from deer eyes to bewilderment, "Fantastic?" she asked.

I excitedly said, "Yeah, fantastic." She quickly came back with, "How do you figure it's fantastic?"

I told her that I had never been to the Las Vegas airport before and I noticed coming in that there was a restaurant that looked pretty good as I was heading to the gate. Since I was going to have a "little" wait I was going to grab my stuff and have dinner. I tell her "thank you" and wish her a great day.

She gets a big smile on her face because she's trying to figure out one or two things, "Is this guy serious? Or is this guy a nut?" Little bit of both probably.

So, I turned and noticed the line that had formed behind me with others who were on the same flight. Now I'm not really a very quiet guy. So, they're all looking at me and what do you think they're doing? Some of them are smiling and grinning, some are kind of snickering because they're trying to figure out the same thing she was, "Is this guy crazy?"

Well as I'm walking past the line of people, two guys literally reached and grabbed me by the arm and they say, "What's this restaurant you're going to?" I told them and they asked, "Well, can we go with you?" By now you probably can guess my reply, "Sure. Come on."

To make a long story not quite so long, I had dinner in an airport with those two guys who before I didn't know and we had a great time. We got to be friends as a matter of a fact we're still friends.

Now, do you think I was really happy about the cancelled flight? Was it really great? Was it really fantastic? But you know, I've got to tell you this, as far as I knew I could have jumped up and down that counter, raised all kind of ruckus and they were not going to fire up a 737 to take me to Tucson. And so, since I couldn't control that, I chose not to fret over it.

A little side note – Do you think that everyone that followed me in that line was in a good mood? Easy right? No way. However, that little lady with the "deer in the headlights look" she was probably more able to deal positively with the people who were behind me. Hopefully the positive "vibes" I was able to leave carried over a little. One thing is for certain I was not going to allow my day to be ruined and two other guys made the same decision.

All this happened because on the flight to Las Vegas, I had a set of headphones on listening to a Zig Ziglar audio and his story about the same thing that happening to him. Classic ripple effect in action.

NOTES

_____

_____

_____

_____

_____

_____

_____

_____

_____

_____

_____

_____

_____

_____

NOTES

NOTES

_____

_____

_____

_____

_____

_____

_____

_____

_____

_____

_____

_____

_____

CHAPTER 3

HABIT 3
Choose to Be Grateful

Choosing to be grateful is really the key to dealing with the difficulty and the people that come along with it. Psychologists have proven the fact that the seeds of depression and the roots of frustration cannot take hold in a grateful heart. Can't happen, so what we have to do is make a decision to be grateful for our blessings.

Not too long ago I saw something that really had an impact. It was a story on CNN's Headline News. The reporter was interviewing a psychologist and the reporter asked, "Okay, during this tough economic time, this historic turbulence, what are some tips that you can give our viewers that will help them psychologically get through what we're going through as a nation?"

The psychologist replies, "You really don't want me to tell them what they need to do."

To which the reporter says, "No. We want you tell them this one. Please share with them what they need to do."

The psychologist reluctantly says, "Okay." She then leans across the news desk and she looks deep into the camera and says, "Turn the television off NOW."

She continued, "Quit watching TV. You must understand that this gentleman's job is to tell you the worst or most salacious thing in the news world to keep you hanging on through the commercials to the next segment. And by the way those commercials are designed to make you discontent with your life by pointing out that your life is, well, terrible – you don't smell right, your hair doesn't look good, you're too old, you're too this or not enough that. Multiple 30 to 60 second snapshots of all the things you don't have, and then we get to the next segment which carries you to the next set of commercials and on and on it goes.

To my surprise she was allowed to go on, "Turn the TV off. Read a good book. Listen to inspirational music or a motivational program. Take a walk. Probably the single most impactful thing many of us could do is to sit down and make a list of things you're grateful for."

After all this the reporter just smiled and said, "Time for a break" and off to commercials they went. Needless to say when the program returned the psychologist was gone.

I thought to myself, "Wow, what great advice."

Now is this the magic pill? Is making a list of things you're grateful for going to fix everything? Of course not but I do believe this, if you are in a dark place emotionally and you sit down at a table, take out a pen and paper then start to make a list of the10 things you are most grateful for, when you stand up you will feel different. You will feel better. Most likely your perspective will change and that dark situation won't seem quite so heavy.

The trick is that every time you start to get that feeling again, pick up that list you made and read it. Maybe add one, two or ten things to it that you missed and again that new perspective on the difficult will likely set in. Just maybe that thing that seemed like a mountain will turn out to really just be a bump in the road.

TAKE ACTION

What are 5 specific things that you are grateful for and why?

1. _____

2. _____

3. _____

4. _____

5. _____

Way to go – Now get up go get a glass of water, take a few minutes then come back and write 5 more.

1. _____

2. _____

3. _____

4. _____

5. _____

What tough situation are you facing right now? Remember it may not be a "big deal" to others but to you it is important. What is it?

_____

_____

_____

Go back and read over your list of things you are grateful for. Think about that tough situation. Has your perspective changed? Can you better cope having begun to inventory your blessings? Write your thoughts below. If you need more room there are note pages in the back of the book.

_____

_____

_____

For each new morning with its light, For rest and shelter of the night, For health and food, for love and friends, For everything Thy goodness sends.
—Ralph Waldo Emerson

BONUS SECTION

I know what some of you are thinking, "I just do not know what I could be thankful for. Things are really tough and I just don't feel very 'thankful' right now."

Listen, I have been right there, at that point where the world seems to be closing in and there "is just nothing to be thankful for." It is at that very moment when there is so very much for which to be grateful. That is when "the list" becomes critical.

One thing you can put right at the top of that list is the fact that you can see and read. Did you know that one in four people worldwide are illiterate and that over 40 million people are completely blind. Not only can you see and read you have the ability to write in the take action sections. When you got up just a moment ago to get a glass of water there were a lot of things to be thankful for there – the ability to stand and walk, the fresh water to drink, if you are at home then you have a home and if you are at work then you have a job. That is at least your first five things.

As for me I remind myself that I have a beautiful wife who loves me and wonderful, healthy children. My health is good and I am blessed with a reasonably good mind. All things that the hustle and bustle of each day will overshadow …if you make the choice to let it.

Choose now to be grateful, choose now to keep that list handy, read and add to it every time the world starts to creep in. Eric Hoffer, recipient of the Presidential Medal of Freedom, in his book *Reflections On The Human Condition,* may have said it best, "The hardest arithmetic to master is that which enables us to count our blessings."

NOTES

_____

_____

_____

_____

_____

_____

_____

_____

_____

_____

_____

_____

_____

NOTES

_____

_____

_____

_____

_____

_____

_____

_____

_____

_____

_____

_____

_____

CHAPTER 4

HABIT 4
Choose to Respond to Life

This just may be the most overlooked strategy in dealing with difficult people and situations. Choose to respond to life, not to react. Sounds simple enough and it is, there is a catch. While simple to conceive choosing to respond and not react is not easy. Actually it goes against our human nature to defend ourselves immediately when confronted.

One of the best explanations of why this is such an important skill to master comes from Jack Canfield. You may not recognize that name but you will certain recognize his work. He is the co-author of the 'Chicken Soup for the Soul' book series.

Not too long ago I got an opportunity to sit down and talk with Jack. During this time he shared a formula with me, "E + R = O." It changed my life. He told me that once we understand the simple fact that Events plus our Response (or Reaction) determines the Outcome then when we can really begin to effectively handle the difficulties that come into our lives.

In most cases we are exactly where we find ourselves as a result of the decisions we make. Our choices regarding the events that occur around us cause an outcome that may or may not result in consequences we desire. You really have a lot more influence over this than you may be giving yourself credit for and I am going to explain how this works.

In the E + R = O formula you have to ask yourself a couple of questions. The first is, "Can I control the events that happen around and to me?" The simple answer is, "No." Question number two, "Can I control the outcomes of the situations I find myself in?" Again, the answer is, "No." However, you can definitely influence it. This is where the "R" comes in. You see when faced with any event, positive or negative, your decision whether to react or respond is all important in getting the outcome you really desire.

I know what you are thinking (probably the same thing I first thought), "What's the difference?" Well, the best analogy I can think of is this, when a doctor prescribes a drug treatment to you and your condition worsens they say you are having a "reaction" and if your body begins to heal and get better they say you are "responding." So remember reaction is bad and response is good.

Dictionary.com defines a reaction as, "resistance or opposition to a force, influence, or movement, to act in a reverse direction or manner" in other words to react is to fight in some form. Response is defined, "to act favorably, to exhibit some action to affect an answer." Simply put it is a positive effort to get the result you desire.

I came to this conclusion, there are things about my life I can control and things I cannot. Those things over which I have no control such as events around me I will not fret over and I will control what I do as a result. Bottom line, I will respond to what happens and work very hard not to have a "knee jerk" emotional reaction.

Okay, sometimes things happen to us that are not pleasant, right? The choice we are all faced with is do we compound the event with a negative reaction or attempt to gain some good results through a thoughtful, positive response. The thing so few of us consider is the "ripple effect" of our choices.

The people around you, co-workers, friends and especially your family, they are watching you and in many cases feeding off your behavior. Like it or not we are all leaders in some respect. Everything we choose to do ... or not do, matters and it matters in ways that we oftentimes never see yet it can affect the lives of those around us for years to come.

TAKE ACTION

Look back and review the "Take Action" steps for Chapters 1, 2 & 3. What new thoughts or "A Ha's" do you have now? Taking ownership of these habits is key to "responding to life" versus reacting. Record your thoughts below.

_____

_____

_____

Think back to an incident that you know you reacted negatively. Now be honest with yourself (there is nobody here but you and me). What could you have done differently?

_____

_____

_____

What should your response have been? What were the consequences of your behavior?

_____

_____

_____

*"Between stimulus and
response is OUR greatest
power– The freedom to chose."
– Steven Covey*

THE CRACKER BARREL STORY

Quick review – Can you control the outcomes of situations? Remember you can influence it but you can't control it. The only thing you can control is your response. Let me tell you that can be hard and it is worth every bit of effort you can muster.

So a great thing happened to my daughter and me not too long ago that perfectly illustrates the point. Everything matters, the things we do and even the things we do not do.

My daughter and I went to Cracker Barrel restaurant in Las Cruces, New Mexico and it was a cold, rainy winter day. For those of you who have never visited a Cracker Barrel it is an oasis of southern home cooking in the southwest for this Georgia boy. Sweet tea, fried chicken, cornbread, turnip greens, cobblers I mean just good food. Now, back to the story.

All these restaurants are the same – long front porches lined with rocking chairs and places where folks can sit down and play checkers. Well, as we are walking up to the door I notice out of the corner of my eye an elderly lady coming down that porch toward the door. Now she was struggling a bit and was walking with the help of one of those big sliver canes. You know the kind, thick handle with 4 padded feet on the bottom

Being a southern gentleman combined with the fact that my grandmother beat a couple of things into me – "Yes, Ma'am,"

"No, Ma'am," "Thank you," "Please," and "You always hold the doors for ladies", I wait for the little old lady so I can open the door for her. I am also thinking that this will be a great example for my daughter.

So as we are standing there in the misty rain shivering and holding the door for this lady. She approaches the door and I smile real big and she smiles real big at me and then snatches the door out of my hand and says, "I can open the door for myself. Thank you very much."

So now, I'm faced with a choice. Here is the moment when we get to see if I really believe what I say all over the country.

My choice is pretty simple. I could kick her cane out from under her and say, "Good luck crip," or I do what I did. We just stepped aside, said, "I'm sorry," and let her go on her way. Now as the door was closing (by the way we were still outside in the cold) my daughter looks up at me and says, "What's that all about?" I replied, "I don't know but what do we do next time?" Then it happened, she looked at me and said confidently, "We open the door because that's what we do."

Wow! Have you ever thought you're going to teach somebody a lesson? Set the great example. I mean I was thinking, "I'm going to set a great example for my daughter. She's going to learn a lesson from this." No, the reality is that my daughter taught me one of the best lessons of life.

The really interesting thing is that I cannot ever recall giving my then 10 year old little girl any instruction about opening doors for people. My son is a different story but not her. The only way she would have ever learned this was by observing my behavior and instruction to her brother.

She taught me that every time I react or respond, she's watching me. Everything I do or don't do, she's watching me. And so, what I learned is this – everything I do affects everything I do and everything I don't do affects everything I do, and others see it. So just remember, people are watching and learning from you.

So as you go forward remember this, your co-workers, friends and family are watching the way you react or respond to events. They're learning lessons from you and if you happen to be the leader in whatever group you find yourself this is multiplied. Regardless others are looking to you for guidance whether you know it or not and whether you believe it or not. That is just the facts.

NOTES

_____

_____

_____

_____

_____

_____

_____

_____

_____

_____

_____

_____

_____

NOTES

_____

_____

_____

_____

_____

_____

_____

_____

_____

_____

_____

_____

_____

NOTES

_____

_____

_____

_____

_____

_____

_____

_____

_____

_____

_____

_____

_____

_____

CHAPTER 5

HABIT 5
Choose to Listen

Robert McCloskey, award winning children's author may have said it best, *"I know that you believe you understand what you think I said, but I'm not sure you realize that what you heard is not what I meant."* Stop, go back and re-read that a couple of times. It took me a couple of times to really understand what he was saying and then to be able to relate it to my past experiences.

The interesting thing for me was the realization he was not only talking to me but also about me. Let me break it down simply. How many times have you been talking with someone else and you knew they were not paying close attention or were preoccupied. Maybe you were sharing instructions or some important information they really needed to know and at the end of your time that other person looked you in the eye and said, "I got it." They walk away and just a short time later a conflict arises because it turns out that they didn't "Get it."

The flip side is when you have been that preoccupied person off on a short mental vacation or thinking about the "big game" while someone was trying to share instruction or information with you. The greatest example I can give personally is when my wife asks me to go to the grocery store and "pick up a few things." It seems that I would always forget something she asked me to get and it usually was the one item she desperately needed above all the others.

Now I am a reasonably intelligent guy and my memory is not completely failed …yet. So I would make a mental note of the items grab my keys and head to the store. About half the time I would miss an item and it would often require a trip back to the store, I mean toilet tissue and cookie dough ice cream can both be necessities – Right?

It occurred to me that if I made a list and then "checked it twice" there was a much better chance that I would not forget any critical items. If I then went to my wife and asked her if I missed anything before leaving for the store the odds of a successful trip and not having to make a return trip were greatly increased. Not to say that there is not still a chance for miscommunication, how was I to know that paper towels meant the Brawny, 6 roll jumbo pack, Pic-a-Size with the Tuscan Pear print.

My grandmother gave me a formula when I was a little boy. When in her words I was "talking just to hear myself talk" she would look at me and say "two plus one Bart." 2 + 1? She would smile and say, "God gave you two ears and one mouth. Now you use them proportionately."

Her point was a very simple one – Listen at least twice as much as you talk. We all tend to want to do like the opposite – we want to talk twice as much as we listen. After all I am the most interesting person in world – right? At least that is what we all seem to think at times.

Remember that the greatest communicators are not necessarily the best speakers. The best communicators are people who listen. Listening to the other person, taking the time to listen and ask questions. Most of all let others finish their thought. Not everyone is as eager to hear what you have to say as you are to say it. So practice 2 + 1. It is truly magic.

A huge part of listening is asking questions to obtain clarity. For me it was as simple as making a list and confirming it with my wife. It may be two to three key points that you really want to be sure your staff understand so as you speak with them you ask questions like, "Bill, could you review that last point with us?" or "Laura, what is your understanding of the new procedure?"

If you are on the receiving end of the information questions could be, "Rafael, may I share my understanding of the new procedure just to be sure I am on the same page?" or "JoAnne, before we go any further can I back up and be sure that I completely understand what is expected?." In this case I can assure you of two things – #1 If there are others involved in this discussion someone is saying a big "Thank You" inside because they were lost. #2 The person delivering the info will greatly appreciate the fact that you have placed a value on their information to the degree that you want to be sure you understand.

Let's talk just a little bit about the greatest threat to being an effective listener and communicator. It is the "Big M" – multi-tasking. The big lie we tell ourselves everyday is that we are excellent multi-taskers. The old saying, "Jack of all trades and master of none" is so very true when it comes to talking with others.

How many times have you been in a conversation with someone and you knew they were not all there, I mean fully engaged. What is worse is when you know they are not paying full attention and they come back from time to time and add to the conversation as if they were listening. Do you find it a little annoying and even disrespectful? You know it every time too, I mean who do they think they are fooling?

Got a question – If you know it every time when someone is mentally on a beach in Hawaii when you are talking with them, why would they not know the same about you? Here is a nugget of wisdom – They know it too? None of us are special in that regard.

So, the rule is "be there", totally when talking with others. Fight the inclination to tune out or multi-task in the middle of a conversation. If you are taking precious time to talk with me then focus on me. I promise to do the same for you.

A little trick I use is to focus on the other person eyes. If you focus on their eyes it is very hard not to pay attention to what they are saying. Just give it a try the next time you are talking with someone. This also engages them and they will naturally focus on what you are saying.

This may sound crazy but when I am in a crowded room and there are a lot of people talking around me and someone walks up and starts talking to me, guess what's going on in my mind? I'm thinking, "Eyeballs, eyeballs." It helps me to maintain focus and block out everything else that is going on. That's my little secret and it works.

TAKE ACTION

What are two questions you can ask of someone you are having a conversation with to be sure you completely understand what they are communicating?

_____

_____

_____

What are three things you can begin to do immediately to be a better listener?

_____

_____

_____

Name a person who you have a particularly difficult time communicating with. What can you do differently from this point to gain better understanding with this person? How can "2 + 1" and being there help?

_____

_____

_____

"Listening is a magnetic and strange thing, a creative force. The friends who listen to us are the ones we move toward. When we are listened to, it creates us, makes us unfold and expand"
– Unknown

THE LAST STORY

I have really enjoyed this walk into the world of dealing with difficult people and situations. Honestly it has been one of the most enriching pursuits I have ever undertaken. Mostly because it has shined a bright light on my own shortcomings and helped me to make valuable course corrections along the way. It has also allowed me to help others find peace with one another which has been the greatest reward. This is a story about one such instance.

I got a call from a client that had a real conflict going on in one of their facilities and asked if I could stop by and check it out. She was a little frustrated with everyone involved and just wanted there to be peace so that the job could get done. The conflict had begun to spill over (as they often do) in to other areas and other employees were beginning to pick sides. Not a productive situation at all.

It was a food service facility with a brand new site manager who had just been promoted and she had in her charge a very experienced staff that had been at the site for several years. When I stopped by to talk with the manager right away I could see that she was a "go-getter" and a stickler about proper procedures being followed.

She had printed key procedures and had the pages laminated and posted in key areas all around the kitchen. Near the oven she had posted the proper cooking temperatures for all the food items as well as the correct methods for taking cooking temperatures of various types of hot food. By the ice machine were the instructions for calibrating thermometers using the ice method. There were logs and instructions everywhere it was really a great thing especially for any new employees who may come in to the site.

For the most part everyone in the kitchen was adhering to the procedures and referencing the various posted procedures with any questions. Everyone except for the head cook and chef, Camilla. You see Camilla had been in that facility for nearly 20 years. She had made it very clear that she knew her job and did not need this "girl" telling her what to do. Are you starting to get the picture? By the way Camilla was and is recognized as the very best at what she does, she is very, very good.

The manager told me, "Yeah, I got this prima donna cook. She does not listen to anybody." She went on, "I'm trying to tell her what to do. We've been at this for more than two months. She just doesn't listen and she will not follow procedures no matter what I do." So I asked permission to talk with the staff and to Camilla, put on my best Sherlock Holmes and went to work.

So I walk out into the kitchen and immediately notice that it is a very well ran site. Like most food service facilities the cook/chef runs the action as far as food preparation and service goes and this was no different. Camilla was keeping everyone in line and production seemed to be going very smoothly. One thing I did notice was that Camilla was delivering instructions to the staff fluently in Spanish, English and even a little "Spanglish."

I approached her and asked if she had a few minutes to talk with me and reluctantly she agreed. The first words she uttered once we started were, "I've been doing this as long as she's been alive and I'm going to do this the way I've been doing it."

My reply was really simple, "I completely understand and I would like to know if it is okay to ask you a couple of questions?" She agreed.

So as we were touring "her" kitchen and I made it a point to compliment her on the job she and the staff were doing. As we approached the ice machine I paused and I asked her, "Camilla, if you don't mind could you tell me how to calibrate these new thermometers you all have?" She smiled and started to tell me, "Well, first you do this," and she starts telling me from memory. For the most part she is right on and when she is finished I commented, "I think the manager really wants everyone to know the posted procedure in case someone new comes in. So what does this posted procedure chart say to do first?"

She starts to argue a bit and I smile and very quietly say, "No, no, seriously. What is step one on the chart?" Again, very quietly and very nice I asked, "What is step number one?" She looks at me and looks down at the floor. She drops her head, a small tear runs down the side of her face and she says, "I …I can't read that." I put my hand on her shoulder leaned in and whispered, "You can't read?" And quietly she said, "I can't read English."

I asked her, "How about Spanish? Do you read Spanish?" She looked up at me and said, "Oh, yeah, perfectly." I smiled real big and said, "Well, that is no problem." I knew how to access the same procedures via the internet in Spanish. We printed them out and posted them right beside the English versions before I left.

Bam! We had almost immediate peace in that kitchen. As a matter of a fact I recently visited that site and the new manager and that cook are becoming best friends and the facility is one of the best run in the southwestern United States.

Two months worth of the conflict could have been avoided if that manager had a different attitude and asked one simple question, "Do you understand this?" or "Is there anything more I can do to help make this happen?" or "Would you show me the procedure?"

Simple. I fixed it in like 5 minutes and they thought I was a miracle worker. It was great and it was easy. It was easy because I just went in there with a different perspective, asked a different question, took a different path, and helped them to change the way they were communicating.

It was great to see and a blessing to everyone.

NOTES

NOTES

_____

_____

_____

_____

_____

_____

_____

_____

_____

_____

_____

_____

_____

BONUS CHAPTER

PUTTING IT ALL INTO ACTION

How would you like the secret to dealing with difficulty, the trick to making it all go away and everything working out the way you want it to every time? What about that hardheaded person who just will not see the error of their ways and just doesn't listen to your great advice? Do you want the secret to making sure that everybody listens to you and hears everything you say? The secret for being sure that there is never any miscommunication ever again. Let me tell you? Do you want it?

So do I, it's frustrating isn't it? I mean you try and try yet there are some people who just don't get it no matter what you do. This is just life and I go back to that sage quote from my grandmother we covered earlier, "Don't let the mess inside someone else's head control what goes on in yours."

The real trick is to understand this really clearly. Control what you can and do not fret what you can't. That is exactly what this "bonus" chapter is about, taking action on controlling your mindset. My good friend, television celebrity and noted motivational speaker James Malinchak told me that success in anything you undertake is a combination of three things and these three things affect everything. They are your mental mind set, your continuous investment in your skill set and then just getting off your assets and making it happen. Nothing happens until you make it happen and getting the result you want hinges on your investing in yourself, period.

> Mind set
> + Skill set
> + Get off your Assets
> **S U C C E S S**

Since you are to this point in the book it is pretty clear that you understand investing in yourself to some degree. You invested capital to purchase it and you have invested time to read it. Congratulations, you are on your way. Now comes the test are you going to take action and, as James, would say "Get off your Assets?"

What follows is a plan that carries a 100% guarantee and will work for you every single time without fail and without question. There is just one little catch – You have to do it!

Legendary business guru Jim Rohn said it so eloquently, "You can't hire someone to do your pushups." Just doesn't work that way.

Now sometimes things can seem a little strange and even crazy, they did to me and they may to you as well. However, what is really crazy? Changing nothing and expecting things to get better or stepping outside your comfort zone and trying something new. Remember you are exactly where you are as a result of the decisions you have made. Maybe it is time to look at some of the decisions of people who are where you want to be and doing a little "copycatting."

The most important habit we have discussed is #2 "Protect Your Attitude." It is worth a re-read right now. In it we covered the importance of having a routine to protect the most important parts of each day – the morning immediately after you wake and the evening just before bed. What follows is my daily routine to develop this habit.

I wake early usually 5:30 AM and sit on the edge of my bed and immediately thank God for another day with my family. Then I stand up and stumble to my bathroom and look at myself in the mirror (the older I get the more scary and comical that site becomes). On my mirror I have a card posted and on this card is written the following phrases;

> **I am in CONTROL of my thinking and how I feel – "I am ALIVE – I am ALERT – I feel GREAT!"**

> **If it is to be it is up to me…I CHOOSE today to be the BEST me I can be!**

> **I truly BELIEVE today will be an AWESOME day…I EXPECT the BEST from everyone around ME!**

So I rub the sleep from my eyes focus and repeat these 3 "affirmations" and I do it 3 times. Each time I raise my volume and poke myself in the chest just so I know for sure that I am talking to me. It can be downright funny and I usually get a chuckle out of it. My day is set on the right course now I just have to keep it there.

I then do whatever personal preparation is necessary for the day – shower, dress, etc. The funny thing is that I find myself repeating these phrases throughout this process, kind of like that song you hear first thing in the morning that you just can't get out of your head. As a matter of fact it is exactly like that I just picked the tune I wanted hear and not the local disk jockey.

Then I sit down somewhere for at least 15 minutes and read something uplifting, something that reminds me that things are bigger than little ole' me. My daily quiet time usually involves a Bible study or reading to help set the tone and keep me on track. There are many inspirational resources readily available at your local library or on the internet.

If my day requires that I drive somewhere then I never leave home without a positive and uplifting CD or audio to listen to during the drive. The car is literally my "university on wheels" as Brian Tracy has called it. I take advantage of that time to build my skill set and strengthen my mind set against the barrage of negativity the world shoves my way. It also prepares me to be that light to others that they so desperately need. Nearly every skill we have discussed in these pages is the result of audio programs that I have invested in over the years.

When in my office I have a unique desktop screen on my computer that reinforces the person I have decided to be. Five simple things, the five habits we have covered are displayed for me to read over and over. This helps me to maintain my mindset throughout the hectic day. Here is how it reads;

I will choose to be my best today.
I will protect my attitude and guard my mind.
I will be grateful for the blessings I have.
I will respond and never react to life.
I will take the time to listen to others and to be there.

When I get home I will watch a little local news because I believe it is important to stay in touch with what is going on in my community. However, I do not leave the television tuned to CNN, Fox or any other "so called" news outlet just to have background. If you are accustomed to doing this here is an idea. Put in one of the audio programs you invested in and let it play in the background or maybe some good upbeat music. The point is you choose what plays not some network executive 2000 miles away.

When it is time to go to bed I take a book with me usually something motivational, something to insure that my sleeping mind will dwell on something positive and good. I never watch the late news because frankly it hasn't changed since 6 o'clock and I am protecting my attitude. The mind never sleeps and your subconscious grinds all night on the last few thoughts you had before sleep. This is very important to realize.

So before bed I go to the bathroom and do the nighttime thing, which for me primarily consists of brushing my teeth, and read my 3 "affirmations" again.

> **I am in CONTROL of my thinking and how I feel – "I am ALIVE – I am ALERT – I feel GREAT !"**

> **If it is to be it is up to me…I CHOOSE today to be the BEST me I can be!**

> **I truly BELIEVE today will be an AWESOME day…I EXPECT the BEST from everyone around ME!**

Then it is off to bed with my book. I read for at least 15 minutes every night and to be honest there are some nights that I am dozing in five and there are some nights I get into it and will read for an hour. The point is that I am committed to 15 minutes.

Mind set

+ Skill set

+ <u>Get off your Assets</u>

S U C C E S S

That's my day and I got to tell you that it is easy and simple. Sure I had to get up 15 minutes earlier in the morning and go to bed a little sooner at night but the return has been no less than fantastic. That is really the only extra investment for you in terms of time. The rest you are already doing, you are just going to change what goes on around you while you do it.

It is a habit and a habit takes 21 days to develop and around 3 to 6 months to set in to the point that it something you just do without really thinking about it. What have you got to lose? What do you have to gain?

Like I said earlier 100% guarantee, it works every time.

The materials and affirmations I use are available at no investment to you on my website – <u>www.bartchristian.com</u> – check it out. There are also regular blog posting and videos that you can access to help you stay on track

Lastly, I want to part with this, we are all given a set amount of time on this Earth and what we do with it is our responsibility. We all have families, friends and co-workers and it is these people that enrich our lives and really make them worth living. You owe them the best that can be given, you also owe it to yourself.

You get what you give or maybe better said by the Apostle Paul, "…whatsoever a man soweth, that shall he also reap." It is inescapable, so the question becomes what are you sowing in life what are you spreading? It is a harvest you look forward to reaping?

If you have found yourself on the road of complaining, fault finding and negativity resolve to change today. It is never too late, there is never too much water that has passed the dam. Make the decision and then work on the habits that will make it a great one.

Choose a new road. Choose to be a good finder. Choose to be an encourager. Simply said, "Choose to be a cheerleader," because cheering works every single time. What you will soon find is that everyone around you will become a cheerleader too. It may be a new road and it is a good road that will ultimately take you to where you want to be. May God bless you with every good thing on this journey called life.

Two roads diverged in a wood, and I—I took the one less traveled by, And that has made all the difference
— Robert Frost

NOTES

NOTES

_____

_____

_____

_____

_____

_____

_____

_____

_____

_____

_____

_____

_____

RESOURCES

WEBSITES

www.bartchristian.com – Downloads and blog updated regularly

www.gimundo.com – Upbeat, positive news site. Funny videos and news stories.

www.goodnewsnetwork.org – Daily news feed of the good happening around the world.

BOOKS

Simple Solutions for Positive Communication – Bart Christian

See You at the Top – Zig Ziglar

Over the Top – Zig Ziglar

Success Principles – Jack Canfield

Success Starts with Attitude – James Malinchak

SCRIPTURE

Book of Psalms – Mostly by David – Great help to understand the human condition.

Proverbs – King Solomon – Excellent life guide for dealing with others.

NOTES

_____

_____

_____

_____

_____

_____

_____

_____

_____

_____

_____

_____

_____

_____

_____

_____

WHO IS BART CHRISTIAN?

Bart Christian is President of
Southwest Training Systems Inc. and
author of
the soon to be released book series
SIMPLE SOLUTIONS

Bart's southern style and subtle humor combined with real world content, enthusiasm, passion and energy with the purpose of making a positive difference in others lives have made him a favorite among many organizations. Being from a small town in Georgia and becoming a self made success has given Bart a real world perspective that relates to all staff levels.

The Simple Solutions series will take the audience from understanding themselves to understanding others. They will learn how to use these skills to become a more effective communicator and to better deal with conflict and difficult people throughout everyday and beyond.

They will discover, as Bart has, that their quality of life is a direct result of their communication and relations with others. Attendees will come away with simple tools that anyone can use and are proven to work in the real world. These easy to follow, step by step principles are what set Bart apart from other speakers.

Bart has a passion for sharing these simple steps with others and audiences will be moved as they begin to understand that they really can have a better quality of life. To date Bart has spoken to thousands of food service staff from Georgia to California on topics of leadership, communication, sanitation and safety.

Bart Christian

The Ideal Choice For A Speaker At Your Next Event!

Programs can be tailored to fit your theme of:

Professional Growth,

Personal Development,

Team Building, Coaching

Staff, Leadership, Change,

Motivating Staff, etc.

To Check Availability or for More Information:

Call: 1(888) 838.1550 or (520) 744.1092

Email: bart@bartchristian.com

www.BartChristian.com

BART'S 5 KEY TOPICS!

Simple Solutions For Communication

(Motivational Keynote 45 or 60 minutes)
(Workshop 90 minutes)

We all need to be reminded that the quality of our lives is a direct result of the quality of the relationships we enjoy with others on the job and at home. This program takes a humorous and energetic look at ourselves and how we interact with others.

Simple Solutions For Dealing with Difficult People

(Motivational Keynote 45 or 60 minutes)
(Workshop 90 minutes)

This insightful message is designed to help the audience recognize non-productive behaviors and actions in others as well as in themselves. We will identify individual purpose and distinguish those things that are just not worth the fight. Also, coping strategies are presented that can make the inevitable difficult situation turn out more positively.

Simple Solutions For Conflict Resolution

(Motivational Keynote 45 or 60 minutes)
(Workshop 90 minutes)

Conflict is inevitable at home, on the job and in our daily lives. How we handle conflict when it comes can determine our quality of life and relationships. This program will explore not only our direct involvement in conflict but also how we can mediate conflicts that arise around us. The audience will learn skills for dealing with personal conflict and mediating conflicts between other co-workers.

Simple Solutions For
Coaching Employees
(Motivational Keynote 45 or 60 minutes)
(Workshop 90 minutes)

The most valuable resource any manager has is their staff. Coaching employees involves not only helping the weakest performers to improve it also includes challenging senior staff to strengthen and expand existing skills. This workshop focuses on skills for building trust, listening, providing feedback nd understanding as well as developing coaching plans for staff.

Simple Solutions For
Leadership
(Motivational Keynote 45 or 60 minutes)
(Workshop 90 minutes)

Effective leadership is a skill that organizations must have to meet the demands of today. This program makes clear the difference between management and leadership. Attendees will learn to recognize and apply leadership practices along with examining different styles. Also how issues such as empowerment, delegation, and motivation are tied directly to leadership.

Programs can be tailored to fit your theme!

FOR MORE INFORMATION:
Call: 1(888) 838.1550 or (520) 744.1092
Email: bart@bartchristian.com
www.BartChristian.com

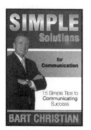

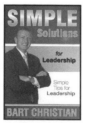

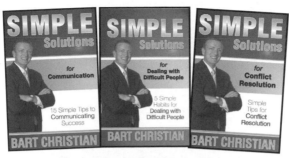

Ask About Special Quantity Discounts

To Place An Order Go To
WWW.BARTCHRISTIAN.COM
Or Call
1-888-838-1550

NOTES
